D1070434

MILLARD FILLMORE

PRESIDENTIAL ✦ LEADERS

MILLARD FILLMORE

ALISON M. BEHNKE

TWENTY-FIRST CENTURY BOOKS/MINNEAPOLIS

To jkca, who always greets me with a happy smile —amb

Twenty-First Century Books
A division of Lerner Publishing Group
241 First Avenue North
Minneapolis, MN 55401 U.S.A.

Website address: www.lernerbooks.com

Library of Congress Cataloging-in-Publication Data

Behnke, Alison.
    Millard Fillmore / by Alison M. Behnke.
        p.   cm. — (Presidential leaders)
    Includes bibliographical references and index.
    ISBN-13: 978–0–8225–1495–4 (lib.bdg. : alk. paper)
    ISBN-10: 0–8225–1495–8 (lib.bdg. : alk. paper)
        1. Fillmore, Millard, 1800–1874—Juvenile literature. 2. Presidents—United States—Biography—Juvenile literature. I. Title. II. Series.
    E427.B44 2007
    973.6'4'092—dc22   2005004330

Manufactured in the United States of America
1 2 3 4 5 6 – JR – 12 11 10 09 08 07

Contents

Carding.

Young Fillmore worked in a mill equipped with wool carding machines (center). The first machines for carding wool were built around 1800. They prepared wool for spinning into yarn. Preparing wool for spinning had previously been a very difficult task. Individuals performed the tedious job by hand, using wire brushes (bottom). Eventually, people invented other machines that could spin and weave wool.

INTRODUCTION

Wherever I can be of most service, there I am willing to go; I seek no distinction but such as may be acquired by a faithful laborer in a good cause. I ask no reward but such as results to all from a good government well administered.
—Millard Fillmore, 1844

The young man stood in a corner of the workshop, his sandy-haired head bent intently over a small book that lay open on the desk. The noise of men's and boys' voices and whirring machinery rang around him. But at this moment, his attention was focused on the words in front of his eyes. Seventeen-year-old Millard Fillmore had a serious task at hand. He was reading the dictionary.

Reaching the end of the entry and holding it in his mind, he rose and returned to the hard, grimy work of an apprentice (student) in a cloth-making mill. As he moved among the carding machines that prepared wool for spinning into yarn, he replayed the word and its definition over and over in his head. When he felt certain that it was fixed in his memory, he stole a few seconds to read another new word. Soon he had learned that one too.

When the workday ended, Millard returned to his room with aching muscles but an eager mind. Lighting the oil lamp, he pulled out his dictionary again. With the few other books that he had, he set about studying late into the night.

Millard Fillmore believed that hard work could accomplish anything—especially in the United States of America. He lived that belief, putting effort into everything he tried. By the time he was a teenager, Millard had already done his share of backbreaking labor on his family's farm. He studied long and hard at school and served as an apprentice for masters both cruel and kind. He went on to work as a teacher and a lawyer and to become a devoted husband and father. As he grew older, he developed a deep patriotism. When he was first elected to public office at the age of twenty-nine, he proved to be an honest politician. He truly believed in his duties as a servant of the people.

Whatever job Millard set for himself, he committed to it with energy and industry. And from his birth in a log cabin to his service as the thirteenth president of the United States, he showed himself and others that determination and hard work could lead from humble beginnings to great success.

CHAPTER ONE

HUMBLE BEGINNINGS

*His light hair was long, his face was round
and chubby, and his demeanor was that of a
bright, intelligent, good natured lad . . . with
an air of thoughtfulness.*
—William Scott, describing
his friend Millard Fillmore in 1814

In 1800 Nathaniel and Phoebe Fillmore were struggling to make ends meet. The young couple's farm in central New York State's Cayuga County was barely producing enough food for them to survive. Bad weather and poor soil plagued their crops. They lived in a simple log cabin that they'd built with their own hands and which they shared with Nathaniel's brother and his family. The home was cozy enough against the winter winds, but it was poor all the same.

The Revolutionary War (1775–1783) had won the American colonies their freedom from Britain. But the war had not been over very long. The new nation was full of excitement and hope. Like many Americans at the time, the Fillmores had journeyed westward after the war. They had traveled from Vermont to seek their fortunes in what was then an unsettled wilderness. So far, Nathaniel and Phoebe had found only hardship. The success and wealth that they had hoped to discover here were still beyond their reach.

But on January 7, 1800, they had reason to celebrate despite their troubles. That night, Phoebe gave birth to the family's second child and first son. In that small, simple cabin, Nathaniel and Phoebe gazed happily at their new baby. They named him Millard—Phoebe's last name before marrying Nathaniel—and they dreamed of a great future for the boy.

SECOND CHANCES AND BIG DREAMS

While Millard was still a toddler, his parents decided to try their luck someplace new. The farm's crops had continued to fail. The bills had continued to pile up—especially as the Fillmore family had continued to grow. They packed up their belongings and moved a few miles northward to the village of Sempronius. In their new home, they rented a farm and a large plot of land. They were sorry not to own their own land anymore. But they were eager for a second chance.

Once again, Nathaniel and Phoebe set about building a life for themselves out of the hard soil and rough wilderness. Nathaniel planted crops, while Phoebe did chores around the house and cared for the children. Yet despite their determination, the odds still seemed stacked against them. They managed to scrape by, but the Fillmore household remained poor.

Nevertheless, Millard was growing up a happy and healthy boy. When he was about seven years old, he started going to school. Each day he walked to a one-room schoolhouse in the town of New Hope. There Amos Castle taught local children to read and write. As Millard later remembered it, the small country school was "an old deserted log house, which had been furnished with a few benches without backs, and a board for writing upon. In this school I learned my alphabet."

Young Millard quickly proved to be an excellent pupil. He fell deeply in love with books and learning. Soon at the head of his class, Millard moved on to a different school to learn more advanced subjects such as math.

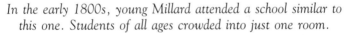

In the early 1800s, young Millard attended a school similar to this one. Students of all ages crowded into just one room.

In addition to being clever, Millard was a popular lad. Although he was less outgoing than many other boys, he was friendly and kind. Some of his fellow students must have envied him a little for the praise his teachers heaped upon him. Nevertheless, he was quick to make friends and good at keeping them. Disliking conflict, he often acted as a schoolyard peacemaker. He tried to treat everyone fairly and with respect, and most often they treated him the same in return.

While Millard did well in school, he could not spend as much time studying as he would have liked. He had other duties. He helped his father and brothers in the fields and did odd jobs for his mother around the house. From plowing the wheat fields to cutting hay and chopping firewood, he did all the chores that were expected of a farm boy.

As the years passed, Millard grew into a fine, broad-shouldered youth. Like other boys his age, he sometimes preferred recreation and sports to farmwork and chores. His father scolded him for wasting his time. As Millard later recalled, "I had, like most boys, a great passion for hunting and fishing, but my father was very unwilling to indulge it." But the boy rarely complained, and hard work never really bothered him. He was good-natured, and he loved his parents dearly.

But Millard was privately ashamed of his family's poverty. Watching his father work so hard for so little reward, he vowed that his own life would be different. Rather than seeing farming in his future, he saw outstanding achievements and fame. He was a realistic young man. He knew that such success would not come to a poor farmer's son easily. But he was more than willing to work for it. So he

Millard was an ambitious young man. He would read anywhere.

⸻ ◇ ⸻

continued to read books on every subject and to learn all that he could, keeping his sights set on big goals all the while.

EARNING HIS KEEP

Even as Millard devoted himself to his studies, his family's poverty stood in his way. With the family still growing, there were simply too many mouths to feed on the farm's small income. (Nathaniel and Phoebe would have nine children in all.) The Fillmores needed extra money. At fourteen years old, Millard was the only son old enough to go to work.

Nathaniel was determined that his sons would not end up as penniless farmers like himself. He found a position for Millard as an apprentice. Boys at that time often served as apprentices to masters of various trades. In return for their work, their masters usually fed them, gave them a place to stay, and taught them how to perform the trade themselves. Millard would be working for a cloth maker. His name was Benjamin Hungerford.

Hungerford's shop was in the town of Sparta. It was many miles from the Fillmore farm. With no means of transportation, Millard walked most of the way. He rode only when a passing cart or wagon driver was friendly enough to give him a lift. Along the way, he must have had plenty of time to think about what lay at the trip's end. He had never been away from home for any length of time before. The idea of living in a new place and working for a

*Many kinds of wagons, carts, and carriages traveled U.S. roads
in the early 1800s. Millard got rides for parts
of his trip to Sparta, New York.*

master whom he had never met had to have been a little frightening. On top of these worries, he was sorry to leave his schoolwork, his fellow students, and his loving family.

But Millard had already shown himself to be good with people and with new tasks. He was bright and unafraid of work, and he was eager to learn skills that would help him make something of himself. These thoughts were enough to give him confidence as he headed toward his new adventure in Sparta.

When Millard arrived on Hungerford's doorstep, he quickly got to work. However, there was not always enough cloth-making business for all the shop's apprentices. To keep them busy, Hungerford would often give them other jobs to do, such as chopping wood. Millard was unhappy at the treatment. He felt that the chores Hungerford assigned were outside of what he'd agreed to in becoming an apprentice. As the weeks wore on, his dissatisfaction grew. He began to think of leaving for home.

One day, Hungerford had instructed him to chop wood. Tired and annoyed, Millard informed his master that he had come to learn a trade, not to chop wood. Nevertheless, he headed out into the woods to do the job. Hungerford approached him to scold him for his words—and probably to beat him for them as well. Millard's anger rose up and overcame him. He stood upon the chopping block, raised his ax above his head, and warned Hungerford that if he threatened him with a beating, he would split him like a piece of wood. This was a rare flash of temper from Millard, who was usually so calm. It was enough to convince Hungerford that it would be unwise to take any chances. He walked away.

Soon afterward, Millard returned to the Fillmore farm. He later regretted his actions, recalling the incident as "an unjustifiable rebellion, or at least . . . my threat of knocking him down was going too far." He added, "My only justification . . . is that I have an inborn hatred of injustice and tyranny which I cannot repress."

BETTER TIMES AHEAD

Back at home in the winter of 1815, Millard needed a new master. He soon became an apprentice to a second cloth maker. He entered a contract to work until the age of twenty. He found a job much closer to home. Millard was able to work at the cloth mill during the summer and fall, when it was busiest, and to help on his father's farm in the spring. During the slow winter months, he even had time to go back to school.

Millard's new master, Zaccheus Cheney, was a great improvement over Hungerford. Millard finally began to receive the hands-on training that he wanted. His hard work and dedication were so impressive that his boss promoted him to be a master workman after about one year. In this position, he was able to pass on some of the more tedious work to newer apprentices. This allowed him to focus on more difficult tasks. He also began keeping the books for the shop. Millard and his employers soon discovered that he had a quick, logical mind that was well suited to the careful work of bookkeeping. He enjoyed gathering facts and putting them into an orderly arrangement.

Millard earned a salary of fifty-five dollars a year at his new job. Most of his pay went to support his family.

But he did have a little spending money—more than he'd ever had before. When he was about seventeen years old, Millard used a few dollars of that money to join a library. At that time, people became members of their local libraries, paying fees in order to check out books. Millard's love of books had not faded in the years since he left school. The range of topics and authors that the library offered thrilled him.

In 1818, during the shop's winter lull, Millard took on a new challenge. He began teaching in a nearby village. Millard proved to be a stern but kind teacher. He soon began earning the respect of the tiny community—as well as his biggest paycheck yet. However, having students showed him that he still had much to learn. He longed to continue his own education. When a new school opened nearby, he decided to attend—even though it meant once again juggling work and study. Early in 1819, nineteen-year-old Millard entered the New Hope Academy.

NEW DIRECTIONS

Eager to enrich his mind, Millard was excited to begin his new classes. He soon found a second good reason to enjoy his schoolwork: his teacher, Abigail Powers. Abigail was the daughter of a local minister, but her father had died shortly after she was born. Like Millard, she had grown up in the New York countryside, and like him, she loved books and learning. She had begun teaching school at the age of sixteen. She was twenty-one years old when Millard became her student. Millard was enchanted by her shining auburn hair and her sparkling blue eyes. He had grown into a handsome young man of nearly six feet tall, with a mop of blond hair and bright blue eyes of his own.

Millard and Abigail, each attracted by the other's quick mind, recognized kindred spirits in each other. Abigail was happy to encourage her student's dedication to study, and Millard admired Abigail's gentle manner. Before long, the two fell in love. They would have liked to marry. But Millard felt strongly that he must not become a husband before he could afford to support a family. Saying good-bye to Abigail, he moved back home to finish his apprenticeship. But he promised his sweetheart that he would come back for her.

✧ ————————
Abigail Powers, Millard's teacher, was a charming woman with a lively intellect.

CHAPTER TWO

THE WORKING WORLD

I came among you a poor and friendless boy.
You kindly took me by the hand, and gave me
your confidence and support. You have
conferred upon me distinction and honor. . . .
If my humble efforts have met your
approbation, I freely admit, that, next to the
approval of my own conscience, it is the highest
reward which I could receive for days of
unceasing toil.
—Millard Fillmore, 1842

Back at his family's home—his parents had moved again, to Montville—Millard thought about his future. He had done well as a cloth-maker's apprentice and was grateful to his master for his training. But Millard decided that cloth making was not the career that he wanted. At nearly twenty years old and still almost penniless, Millard had few options. Nevertheless, he had set his sights on a new goal: studying law. In those times, a young man wishing to become a lawyer found a position similar to an apprenticeship. He usually worked as a clerk for an established lawyer, while reading law books and learning from his employer.

Nathaniel Fillmore was proud of his oldest son's ambition. And, recognizing in Millard the strong will to succeed, he decided he would try to find an opportunity for him. When Nathaniel met a local judge named Walter Wood, he saw his chance. He asked Judge Wood to take Millard on as a law student for the springtime months, while Millard still had some time off from Cheney's shop. The judge agreed. Nathaniel surprised Millard with the news at the dinner table. The young man was so overcome with emotion that he burst into tears and rushed out of the room in embarrassment.

Millard began his studies with Judge Wood almost immediately. He spent most of his time reading thick law books. He sometimes ran errands or did little jobs for the judge. As always, he showed himself to be a hard worker and a quick learner. He impressed Wood. In fact, when the springtime trial period ended, the judge invited his young student to stay on and begin a clerkship and study law.

The proposal was very exciting. Here at last was Millard's opportunity to begin a career. But while he dearly wanted to say yes, he still had several months left of his cloth-making apprenticeship. He felt guilty about breaking the promise he had made to Cheney. On top of that, as a law clerk and student—a position that usually lasted seven years—he would have to pay for his room and board. That would cost money that he didn't have.

Millard studied law in Wood's office, built in 1812, in Montville, New York. This photo of the structure was taken after Fillmore died in 1874.

─────────────── ✧ ───────────────

When Millard admitted this difficulty, Wood offered to help right away. He said that he could find work for Millard to help pay his way. He could also lend his student any extra money that he might need. In the end, Millard simply couldn't turn his back on the deal. He approached Cheney and asked to pay him for the time that he still owed. His master agreed, and Millard prepared to stay at Judge Wood's office and to follow the new path that he had chosen.

Millard dressed well for his new position as a law student.
✧ —————————————

THE LAWYER-TO-BE

Hoping to borrow as little money from Wood as possible, Millard returned to teaching school in the winter of 1820. During these months before settling into his clerkship, he continued to read law books in the evenings. And when he arrived back at Wood's office, he was dressed the part of the attorney-in-training, wearing a suit instead of the rougher clothes he'd been used to.

As Millard plunged into his studies, he also tried to earn some money so that he would not need to borrow from Wood. He did not want to owe his teacher. He continued to teach when he could spare the time, and he took odd jobs that came his way. A little more than one year after Millard had joined Wood's office, a local farmer asked the young law student to handle a small legal case for him.

The fee for his services would be three dollars. Millard happily took the job.

Millard did not mention the case to Wood. When the judge heard about it, he became angry with his clerk. Wood claimed that taking the case—especially without informing his employer and teacher—was beneath Millard and had been unprofessional. The money was not worth it, Wood said, and Millard should not have accepted it.

Until this point, Wood had been a kind and thoughtful teacher. Millard had been his devoted pupil. But the suggestion that he should have turned down an opportunity to earn money that he needed so badly bothered the poverty-stricken student. He began to think that perhaps the judge was actually trying to keep him in debt. What if, Millard wondered, the judge were "more anxious to keep [him] in a state of dependence and use [him] . . . than to make a lawyer out of [him]?" At this idea—which may or may not have been true—Millard's hatred for injustice rose up once again. He and his master argued bitterly, ending with Millard's resignation and departure.

Just as he had looked back regretfully on his nearly bloody encounter with Hungerford, Millard later admitted that the experience with the judge could have been a misunderstanding. "I don't think Judge Wood knew, or could realize," he said, "how important three dollars were to me in those days."

MAN-ABOUT-TOWN

While Millard had been working at Judge Wood's office, his family had moved yet again, settling in East Aurora. Millard joined them there. His future had become uncertain. What if his rash actions had cost him his career—or even his chances of marrying Abigail, who still waited for him in New Hope? That winter, while he thought about what to do, he turned back to teaching to earn money.

Millard did not have to wonder about his future for long. Within a few months, he found work with a local justice of the peace (an official who handles small legal matters). The justice gave him several cases to handle. He also helped him continue his law lessons. Relieved at his lucky break, Millard devoted himself to work and study with more determination than ever. However, he soon saw that he could improve his chances of finding work by leaving the small town of East Aurora for a bigger city. Fortunately for him, Buffalo—one of the state's largest cities—lay fewer than twenty miles away. Millard packed up a few belongings and struck out on yet another adventure.

Millard's move to Buffalo, New York, in 1822 offered him many opportunities to develop his career as a lawyer.

Millard arrived in Buffalo in the spring of 1822. He had been there once before, about four years earlier. On that trip, he had walked most of the 140 miles from home to visit relatives and to see a bit of the world beyond his parents' farm. Buffalo had been little more than a country town then. But in the 1820s, it was growing into a busy center of business and industry. And as home to more than two thousand people, it was by far the largest city Millard had ever visited. To the young man, who arrived without knowing a soul and with only four dollars to his name, the city was bursting with excitement.

Millard soon found a teaching job that would pay his bills while he looked for work in the legal field. By summer he had taken a position as a law clerk at the offices of Asa Rice and Joseph Clary. He took up his studies as diligently as ever. Meanwhile, he continued teaching to cover his expenses.

As before, it was very important to Millard to stay out of debt. Even though Buffalo was a lively place, full of restaurants and taverns, Millard was sure to live within his means. Before long, his careful habits and dedication to work had earned him a good reputation around town. In fact, one early biographer commented that "it was no uncommon remark among the young students in the city at that time, at the exhibition of unusual [effort] on the part of a fellow student, that he was as studious as Fillmore."

Millard was also known for being polite, friendly, and blessed with good common sense. All of these traits impressed his fellow Buffalonians. Legend has it that another saying showing his popularity also became familiar: "If Millard Fillmore goes for it, so do I."

Finally, Millard's time and efforts paid off. In 1823 he took a test of his legal knowledge. He passed and joined the bar, allowing him to practice law in New York State.

SETTING UP SHOP

With one of his greatest goals achieved at last, Millard had an important decision to make. Where would he set up his law practice? Buffalo offered many clients and business opportunities. It was also full of eager young lawyers like himself, in addition to older and more experienced attorneys. Doubting his ability to compete with so many other candidates, Millard decided that his chances would be better back in East Aurora. He returned there and opened a small office near the center of town.

Millard began his career with his typical determination. His hard work soon led to good results. Locals heard of the new lawyer, who was said to treat every case—no matter how small—with the utmost care. His practice grew quickly. He also set about the task of building a small law library. His collection gradually grew to contain more than one hundred legal books.

Despite his fairly rapid climb to local success, the lack of self-confidence that had led Millard back to East Aurora remained. This characteristic sometimes threatened to undo his labors, as he could appear timid on occasion. Even after the townspeople invited him to give the Independence Day address, he remained uncertain of his worthiness. In his speech, he admitted to his audience that he "always trod the humble walks of life . . . and [nothing] but a full faith in your charity and generosity could inspire him with confidence to attempt to address you on this important occasion."

Like Judge Wood, Millard practiced law from a modest building. His office (center) was in East Aurora, New York.

———————————————— ✧ ————————————————

But in the winter of 1826, Millard took a big step. All this time, he and Abigail had been writing to each other, continuing their relationship through their letters. Poverty and other obstacles had prevented them from visiting each other often. At times they went for months without seeing each other. Millard had missed Abigail but still felt that he should not marry until he could earn a decent living. As he worked toward this end, the thought of his beloved Abigail gave him even greater desire to succeed. Finally, after more than six years of courtship, he boarded a stagecoach and arrived at Abigail's family home in Moravia.

Some of Abigail's relatives were reluctant to agree to the wedding. Although the Powers were not rich, they traveled in higher social circles than the Fillmores. Some of them thought Abigail was too good for a simple farmer's son— even if he had become a lawyer. But Abigail loved Millard and knew that he was a kind, intelligent, and ambitious man. The couple married at Abigail's brother's house on February 5, 1826. That same night, Millard and Abigail left for East Aurora to begin their life together.

GROWING FAMILY, GLOWING FUTURE

With Abigail by his side at last, Millard worked harder than ever. As a lawyer, he was not a great speaker. However, he was organized and skilled at research. He was also passionate about upholding the Constitution. He cared deeply about seeing justice done. Millard would even turn down cases in which he felt he would be on the wrong side. These qualities impressed his clients, colleagues, and superiors alike. He was soon qualified to try cases before the New York State Supreme Court. More and more business came his way, until he had so many clients that he needed help around the office. He hired a family friend, Nathan K. Hall, as his student and clerk—the same position that Millard had held not many years ago.

Meanwhile, Abigail found a teaching job in East Aurora. With their combined incomes, the two of them were able to afford a small house within a year or so of their marriage. Moving out of Millard's parents' farmhouse, where they had lived temporarily after the wedding, they happily settled into their new home. The pleasant little cottage had shuttered windows and a small, white porch. It sat right across the

In 1826 Millard and some of his friends built this home for Abigail in East Aurora, New York. It is the only home in the United States that was built by the personal labor of a future U.S. president.

———————————————— ✧ ————————————————

street from Millard's office and near many of the town's other businesses.

The cheerful household soon grew even happier with the birth of Millard and Abigail's first child. Millard Powers Fillmore—whom the couple came to call Powers—was born on April 25, 1828. Like Nathaniel and Phoebe Fillmore twenty-eight years earlier, Millard and Abigail Fillmore were filled with joy—and hope—at the sight of their son.

THE
LEVEL AND THE SQUARE.

By the eminent Masonic Poet, ROB MORRIS. This Song and Burns's Adieu to his Lodge, are the finest productions in the Masonic Order.

We meet upon the Level, and we part upon the Square,
What words of precious meaning those words Masonic are,
Come let us contemplate them, they are worthy of our thought,
With the highest and the lowest and the rarest they are fraught.

We *meet upon the Level,* though from every station come,
The king from out his palace, and the poor man from his home ;
For the one must leave his diadem outside the mason's door,
And the other finds his true respect upon the chequered floor.

We part upon the Square, for the world must have its due,
We mingle with its multitude, a cold unfriendly crew ;
But the influence of our gatherings in memory is green,
And we long *upon the level* to renew the happy scene.

There's a world where all are equal—we are hurrying towards it fast,
We shall *meet upon the level* there, when the gates of death are passed,
We shall stand before the Orient, and our Master will be there,
To try the blocks we offer by his own unerring Square.

We shall *meet upon the level* there, but never thence depart,
There's a mansion—'tis all ready for each trusting faithful heart,
There's a mansion and a welcome, and a multitude is there
Who have met *upon the level,* and been tried *upon the square.*

Let us meet *upon the level* then, while laboring patient here,
Let us meet and let us labor, though the labor seem severe,
Already in the western sky the signs bid us prepare
To gather up our working tools, and *part upon the square.*

Hands round, ye faithful masons, form the bright fraternal chain,
We part *upon the square* below to meet in heaven again,
Oh what words of precious meaning those words masonic are—
" We meet upon the level, and we part upon the square,"

H. DE MARSAN, Publisher,
60 Chatham Street, New-York.

This song from the mid-1800s is about two Masonic symbols, the level and the square. The Masons are members of a secret society dating back hundreds of years. Fillmore ran for office as an Anti-Mason.

CHAPTER THREE

PRACTICE AND POLITICS

The law is the only sure protection of the weak, and the only efficient restraint upon the strong. When impartially and faithfully administered, none is beneath its protection, and none above its control.
—Millard Fillmore, 1850

As an increasingly well-known citizen of East Aurora, Fillmore began to get involved in local politics. Throughout New York State, one of the hottest topics of the day was the political battle between the Masons and the Anti-Masons.

The Masons—officially known as the Ancient Free and Accepted Masons—were members of a secret society dating back hundreds of years. While they were not technically a political organization, many of the country's most powerful politicians and businesspeople were members of the group. This fact, combined with their secret rules and meetings, led many people to believe that the Masons had considerable influence in the political world.

Then, in the late 1820s, a former Mason, Captain William Morgan, mysteriously disappeared from his home in Batavia, New York. Before his disappearance, Morgan had had a falling out with fellow Masons. In retaliation, he had threatened to reveal the Masonic Order's secrets. When he vanished, people began to spread rumors that Morgan had been murdered and that the crime was linked to the Masons themselves. The stories led many New Yorkers to suspect that the Masons' power allowed them to operate outside of the law.

The Anti-Masonic Party had formed out of the Morgan scandal. One of the group's earliest and most active leaders was Thurlow Weed. Weed was a newspaper writer and editor who was deeply involved and influential in New York

✧ ———————————
Thurlow Weed edited the
Anti-Masonic Enquirer
newspaper from 1828
to 1830.

Great Meeting!

DEMOCRATIC ANTI-MASONIC
YOUNG MEN'S
COUNTY CONVENTION.

The headline of this poster announces an anti-Masonic convention.
It was held in Genesee County, New York, on October 18, 1832.

———————————————— ✦ ————————————————

politics. He hoped to use the party to prevent Masons from holding political office. Soon more and more people began responding to the Anti-Masons' message. Poor voters liked the party's opposition to the traditional power of the rich Masons. And political hopefuls noticed the fact that the party was winning elections. The movement soon spread beyond New York into other states.

As the Anti-Masons grew, many party members also hoped to ensure that no one—Masons or anyone else— could ignore the law because of wealth or power. This goal appealed to Fillmore's belief in the law's absolute impor-tance and drew him into the world of politics. By the sum-mer of 1828, he was regularly attending Anti-Masonic conventions held around New York. Soon he was heavily involved in the details of state politics.

That fall Fillmore's young political career took a great leap forward. His fellow Anti-Masons chose him to run for election to the New York State Assembly. He accepted the nomination. On November 13, 1828, he won a seat as the representative from Erie County. Saying good-bye to Abigail

Fillmore's early political career included representing Erie County, his home district, in the New York State Assembly. The assembly met in this capitol building in Albany.

⸻ ✧ ⸻

and little Powers in December, he traveled to the state capital of Albany to take his place on the assembly.

THE YOUNG ASSEMBLYMAN

Fillmore arrived in Albany, then the second-largest city in New York, in late December or early January. Just as he had shown up for work at Judge Wood's in new clothes, he appeared on the streets of Albany sharply dressed. He wore a stovepipe, the tall black hat that was then in fashion, and he carried a stylish walking stick. He was eager to make a good impression on his fellow assemblymen. But he knew that he had a lot to learn. Most of the politicians in the capital had much more experience than this twenty-nine-year-old farmer's son. Nevertheless,

Fillmore approached the new job with his usual willingness to work and to learn. He also went into the job with a keen awareness of his duties as a representative of the people.

During the assembly's session, Fillmore spent more time listening than actively taking part. He was timid about his inexperience. He also missed Abigail a great deal and eagerly awaited her letters. In them, she expressed her own loneliness for him. In January 1829, she wrote:

> *Your society is all I have thought of. O, that you could have been here to have studied with me, you have been scarcely out of my mind during the day. . . . I will now bid good night to my kindest and tenderest friend, with the most sincere and ardent wish for his health, happiness, and satisfaction . . . a thousand blessings upon you, may you sleep sweetly with the image of your Abigail hovering over you.*

Fillmore was determined to make his time away from home and family as useful as possible. He carefully studied the assembly's proceedings and absorbed everything that he could. He also joined one committee. While he was quiet there too, it gave him the chance to see another part of the system. When his term ended in the spring, he went home feeling more confident in his understanding of his state government and the way it worked.

He was not home with Abigail and Powers for long. His local popularity and his support of the Anti-Masons won him reelection to the assembly in November 1829. He returned to Albany for another term. This time he played a larger role in both the general assembly and the committees. He spoke up against the Masonic Order, in support of small businesses in New York State and on behalf of his party.

By the end of his second term in the assembly, Fillmore was becoming a respected politician. The *Albany Evening Journal* described him as having "all the . . . judgment of an experienced man. . . . He exhibits . . . a mildness . . . of temper, mingled with firmness of purpose, that is seldom [found] in the same individual . . . there is in his manner an indescribable something which creates a strong impression in his favor."

But despite Fillmore's political success, the session had also been a difficult time in some ways. He had been homesick for Abigail again. Adding to his sadness had been the deaths of a friend and of one of his brothers. He happily returned to Abigail, to Powers—who by now was almost two years old—and to their little home.

A CHANGE OF SCENERY

Millard Fillmore had completed two terms of public office, was the head of a growing family, and ran a legal practice that was going strong. He and Abigail were content in East Aurora. But with both his legal and political careers going so well, Fillmore couldn't help but wonder if he might finally be ready to compete in Buffalo.

In the spring of 1830, he and Abigail took the plunge. The Fillmore family moved to Buffalo. They soon found a comfortable two-story house. Painted white with green shutters and surrounded by a picket fence, it sat in a good location not far from Main Street. Fillmore took care of the business of moving his law practice to Buffalo and finding new clients. Abigail settled the family into their new home. She found a hobby in gardening. Her roses, geraniums, and other flowers soon gained the admiration of her fellow Buffalonians. And although she had stopped teaching school after Powers's birth, she continued to keep her mind active by studying French and by playing the piano. She also continued to read as much as possible. The couple collected as many books as they could. Fillmore always brought home new additions after his trips away. Their personal library contained hundreds of books.

That November Fillmore left his home and business once more for a third term in the state assembly. By this time, he was a well-respected and popular representative. The 1831 session was relatively quiet. However, Fillmore had the chance to distinguish himself by introducing a bill (law) that was deeply important to the interests of the working people of New York.

At that time, people who owed money and could not repay their debts on time could be arrested and put in prison. This rule was in effect all across the country. Creditors—the people to whom the money was owed—said that it was necessary to protect their investments. But the law also had critics. Building jails was expensive to the state and to taxpayers. And debtors had little chance to repay their debts while in prison. This often left families in hard situations.

The law had become a major point of controversy. Fillmore, as someone who had known poverty, sympathized with workers. They claimed that the law discriminated against people who were not born into wealth. He also believed that the law hurt the state by making people afraid to start small businesses. After careful research and preparation, he helped write and present a bill that would, he hoped, satisfy both average workers and the rich creditors.

The bill proposed replacing the imprisonment rule with one on bankruptcy. The new law would give people the chance to declare bankruptcy when they found it absolutely impossible to pay off their debt. However, it also protected creditors and their money by making it illegal to fake bankruptcy.

The bill faced opposition from some members of the assembly. The old law had been in place a long time. Many politicians were reluctant to change it. The creditors who benefited from the rule were much more powerful than the debtors who suffered because of it. But Fillmore fought hard to get his bill passed. He argued that it benefited borrowers and lenders alike. As he had shown in his work as a lawyer, Fillmore's style of speaking was not impassioned. It was extremely logical and straightforward. In addition to

In 1831 Fillmore left Albany (above), proud of the bankruptcy law he had introduced in the New York State Assembly.

his clear and sensible arguments, his good standing among his fellow assemblymen helped his cause. Finally, on April 2, 1831, the assembly passed the bill.

Fillmore was proud of the new law. And his effort on behalf of common working folks helped to reinforce his reputation as a "man of the people." But the same day that brought Fillmore this success also brought him deep sorrow. On April 2, his mother died of an illness called dropsy (swelling of the body caused by fluid retention). She was only fifty years old.

BUFFALONIANS

Back home in Buffalo that spring, Fillmore continued to establish himself as a prominent citizen of his new hometown. He need not have worried about his business's success. It thrived in the new setting. Meanwhile, he and Abigail took part in the many social opportunities that Buffalo offered. They went to dinners, parties, plays, and concerts. Townspeople continued to admire Fillmore's politeness, especially toward women. Although women were not allowed to vote then, many people liked to say that if women could vote, Fillmore would win every election. But he doted on no one as much as his dear Abigail. Other wives often commented on how attentive he was to her. They told stories about times such as the night when, on arriving at a friend's house, he escorted Abigail inside. Then he hurried back home to pick up flowers that she had arranged earlier that day and forgotten to bring with her.

The Fillmores continued to be active in causes close to their hearts, such as education and public libraries. They also joined the large Unitarian church in town.

LOCAL PRIDE

The Fillmores' new hometown was a young city. In fact, it was a few years younger than Fillmore himself. Originally founded in about 1803, the village of Buffalo sat alongside Lake Erie in far western New York. During the War of 1812 (1812–1815), British troops captured the settlement and burned it to the ground. The recovery from that destruction had been slow and difficult.

However, things turned around in 1825 when the Erie Canal was completed. Extending between the Hudson River to the east and Buffalo, the canal provided the final link in a continuous inland water route from the Atlantic Ocean to the Great Lakes. Many people praised the canal as an engineering triumph and an economic blessing. Buffalo's fortunes exploded as the small town suddenly became a center of shipping and industry. Its population exploded as well, growing from about twenty-four hundred people in 1825 to ten thousand in 1832. Called a "gateway to the West," Buffalo offered Fillmore a wealth of opportunities and possibilities. In return, he did all he could to win support and funding for improvements to Buffalo during his time in state and federal office. Fillmore considered himself a devoted Buffalonian, and the people of Buffalo were proud to count him as one of their own.

✧ —————————

Horses or mules pulled heavy barges loaded with goods and passengers along the Erie Canal.

Meanwhile, Fillmore took his longest break from office in almost three years. While he missed public service, he was surely glad to be at home for the birth of the Fillmores' second child, Mary Abigail, on March 27, 1832. Nicknamed Abby, the little girl was a joyful addition to the Fillmore household.

As always, though, Fillmore's stay at home was shorter than he expected. In November 1832, he was elected for the first time to national office as a member of the House of Representatives in the U.S. Congress. Knowing that he would soon be away in Washington, D.C., he invited his legal clerk, Nathan K. Hall, to become his partner in the law firm. Hall accepted. Fillmore left in December, confident that the business was in good hands. He was sorry, as ever, to leave Abigail, their son, and their new daughter. But he knew that the job he'd been chosen by the people to do was important. He traveled to the nation's capital looking forward to the new experience that lay ahead.

Fillmore went to Washington, D.C., to serve in the House of Representatives for the 1833 session.

CHAPTER FOUR

NATIONALLY KNOWN

*My maxim has always been that individuals
have no claim upon the public for official
favors, but that the public has a right to the
service of any and all of its citizens.*
—Millard Fillmore, 1844

Fillmore arrived in Washington, D.C., feeling similar to the way he had felt when he'd begun his first term in the New York assembly. Although he'd gained political experience, the national stage was still a big step. However, he was lucky enough to meet the famous senator and talented speaker Daniel Webster. The acquaintance soon made him feel more comfortable.

Fillmore soon had much more than his own nervousness to think about. The 1833 session of Congress was lively. The president was Andrew Jackson, who had won the presidency in 1828 and again in 1832. Jackson was popular, but he was also controversial. His fiery temper, along

with some of his policies, earned him firm enemies—
among them Fillmore's new friend Webster and Senator
Henry Clay of Kentucky. Jackson led the Democratic Party.
His opponents in both the Anti-Masons and in the
National Republican Party vowed to fight the Democrats
and Jackson on a variety of issues. One major controversy
surrounded Jackson's effort to shut down the national bank.
He had succeeded in 1832, but tensions lingered. In addition, Jackson's foes frequently accused him of abusing his
presidential authority. The showdowns with President

*Senator Henry Clay (standing, center) addresses the Senate. Fillmore's
powerful friend Senator Daniel Webster is seated to Clay's left.
Both men were persuasive speakers.*

This cartoon shows the columns of the Bank of the United States crashing as President Jackson (right), who served from 1829 to 1837, triumphs. His success at closing the bank did not last.

Jackson made Fillmore's first visit to the capital an exciting one. However, as he had during his first trip to Albany, he kept largely to the wings, watching and learning.

By the time Fillmore's first congressional term ended in December 1834, the Anti-Masonic Party had begun to falter. The uproar over the Morgan scandal had long since died down. The party was not as successful as it had been in earlier elections. The Anti-Masons had tried joining forces with the National Republican Party. This effort was based mostly on their shared opposition to Jackson and the Democrats. As a result, while Fillmore still considered himself an Anti-Mason, he had won many National Republican votes in his election to the 1831 New York assembly, as well as in his election to Congress.

The Anti-Masonic Party eventually disappeared. Its members decided to form a new political group. The new Whig Party was the outcome of this decision. Many members of the National Republicans and other, smaller groups joined the Whigs as well. Some Democrats, driven away by what they saw as Jackson's abuse of his power, even crossed over to the Whig cause.

Eager to see the new party succeed, Fillmore decided not to run for another term in Congress. Instead, he went home to Buffalo and began working to bring together Anti-Masons and National Republicans in support of the Whigs. He attended many political meetings. He spread the Whigs' message to voters in the city and beyond. His good reputation helped convince many New Yorkers to join the party. Fillmore and other former Anti-Masons also worked hard to support Whig candidates in local and national elections.

Fillmore also returned to his law practice, which was still growing. In January 1836, with the addition of Solomon G. Haven, the partnership became Fillmore, Hall, and Haven. Before long it was one of the most well-respected law firms in all of western New York. The three talented lawyers had different styles that worked well together. Fillmore also continued to expand the firm. He hired clerks and instructed them in the law, as Fillmore himself had been instructed.

RETURN TO WASHINGTON

After his two-year absence from Congress, Fillmore ran for reelection as the Whig candidate in 1836. He won the election in November and headed back to Washington in early 1837. On this trip, Abigail joined him in the capital for the first time. She stayed with him there through most of the term. Abigail closely followed current events, and her husband often asked for her advice. She also attended social outings in Washington, as many congressional wives did. But she liked small gatherings and intimate discussions better than big parties. The Fillmores were happy to be with each other. However, they deeply missed Powers and Abby, whom they had left in the care of relatives. They felt that New York—filled with friends, family, good schools, and broad open spaces—was a better place for children than Washington.

————————✧
Abigail went to Washington, D.C., with Fillmore for the first time in 1837.

"YOUR AFFECTIONATE FATHER, MILLARD FILLMORE"

Whenever either of the Fillmore parents was away from their children, they wrote many letters to stay in touch, just as they did when they were apart from each other. Fillmore once wrote to his son remarking on the value of letters, saying,

> If we could not write, you could hardly hear from me during all the time I am away from home . . . you would feel great anxiety about me and so should I about you. But now by this extraordinary act, I can take a little bundle of thoughts . . . and send them to you as well as though I told them to you in a private room by ourselves. This is a very great privilege. Did you ever think of it before?

As former teachers with deep feelings on the power of reading and writing, both mother and father tended to correct their son's and daughter's grammar and spelling. But the Fillmores also used their letters to share stories and advice with their children. They passed along their belief in hard work and perseverance, expressed by Fillmore's comment to Abby that "every person should have some profession or trade. . . . Nothing is so degrading as beggary and nothing so painful as dependence." To Powers he wrote, "Whenever . . . you do not know exactly what to do, do the best you can and you will succeed."

As the children grew older, their correspondence with their parents also covered topics including history, literature, foreign languages, religion, art, and astronomy.

Both Abigail and Millard cherished the mail they received
from home. When Fillmore was especially proud of a letter
from Powers or Abby, he would show it to fellow
congressmen or to Washington women. And the letters
served as the loving family's closest contact throughout
their periodic separations. As Fillmore wrote to Abby while
he was alone in the capital one winter, "I have dreamed
many times of being home and seeing you and
your...brother and your good Ma and I hope soon to have
this pleasure in reality."

*The Fillmore family's mail would have traveled by a stagecoach
such as this one or by horseback or by steamboat. After
1838 railroads could officially carry U.S. mail too.*

The Democrat Martin Van Buren—who had formerly served as Jackson's vice president—had become president. Like Jackson, Van Buren had many foes, who particularly disliked his opinion on banks. Van Buren had followed in Jackson's footsteps by revising the national banking system. When a widespread economic downturn, known as a depression, struck in 1837, people largely blamed Van Buren. The Whig Party benefited from the unpopularity of the Democrats. In addition, New York businesspeople

This detail from a political cartoon, published during Van Buren's presidency (1837–1841), proposes that Andrew Jackson (left) used hypnosis to get Van Buren to maintain Jackson's banking policies. The crown and scepter (right) are a reference to the unpopular, kinglike views of both men about this and other issues.

needing legal help during the crisis flocked to Fillmore, Hall, and Haven. Nevertheless, it pained Fillmore to see his fellow Americans struggle. He said that "lawyers may perhaps make money in such times, but to them they are unpleasant when they see the ruin of businessmen."

Even in the midst of the depression, another issue soon took center stage and also brought Fillmore into the spotlight. Many Americans—including Fillmore—felt strongly that the U.S. Army was not prepared to defend the country from an attack. The presence of British troops in Canada fed this suspicion. Canadians who opposed British control began organizing uprisings, which Americans across the border sometimes supported. In late December 1837,

——————— ✧

Canadian rebel leaders such as Louis Joseph Papineau (right) asked Americans to help fight British rule in Canada. But American leaders worried that the U.S. Army could not defend the United States against the British.

British forces crossed into New York State and set fire to the *Caroline*. This U.S. steamship had been carrying weapons and supplies to the rebels. At least one American died, and the British destroyed the ship—sending it drifting down the Niagara River in flames.

As stories of the attack spread, some Americans exaggerated their reports. They said vicious things about the British. The incident spurred an outcry by Americans, who demanded that the president declare war on Britain. Van Buren—along with many members of Congress—was determined to defend both the northern border and the nation's honor. But they were also reluctant to endanger relations with Britain. The two nations had been relatively friendly since the end of the War of 1812. They had an agreement stating that neither would interfere in the activities of the other. In the congressional debate that followed the *Caroline* attack, Fillmore was outspoken. He argued for a balance among peace, national defense, and international relations. He proposed several resolutions and amendments in pursuit of this goal. His strong position on the issue gained him widespread attention in Congress. It also highlighted his patriotism—a feeling that had grown in him ever since he had begun serving as an elected representative.

UPS AND DOWNS

Fillmore's supporters reelected him to Congress in 1838. The Whig Party had done well in many of the year's elections, even gaining the governor's seat. Fillmore found himself with more party colleagues in Washington than ever before. Whig hopes rose even higher in late 1839 when the party nominated William Henry Harrison for president.

Harrison, who had gained fame by fighting Native Americans in the Battle of Tippecanoe, seemed to have a good shot at victory. He ran with John Tyler as vice president. Harrison-Tyler slogans in the race against Van Buren included "Tippecanoe and Tyler Too" and "Farewell Dear Van Not the Man."

Harrison (seated on horse) *became known as Tippecanoe after burning Prophetstown, a Native American community on the Tippecanoe River in Indiana Territory. This 1811 event subsequently became known as the Battle of Tippecanoe.*

The Whigs' high hopes proved justified in December 1840 when Harrison won. Fillmore was reelected to Congress, and a wave of Whigs swept into Washington once more. Fillmore won the important job of chairman of the House of Representatives Ways and Means Committee. This group deals with economic policy and other significant matters. Another party member held the position of Speaker of the House. The Speaker of the House, as its leader, is the most important member of Congress. Whigs were feeling optimistic about the coming four years.

But in April 1841, tragedy suddenly struck. Taken ill with a severe case of pneumonia, Harrison died after just one month in office. Tyler was hurriedly sworn in as

✧ ————————

Mourners gather around Harrison's deathbed in 1841. With his death in office, a vice president was called to Washington to replace a president for the first time.

president amidst an atmosphere of shock and grief, while the Whigs struggled to put things back together. But despite the chaotic start to his term, President Tyler proved soon enough that he had ideas of his own. He vetoed (refused to approve) the bills supported by his party. By doing so, he went against Whig plans—in particular, changes in banking that Whigs hoped would end the economic depression. Tyler soon alienated himself from the Whig Party. Eventually all but one of his close advisers resigned in outrage.

Nevertheless, Fillmore and other Whigs still worked to achieve their goals. They wanted to counteract what they saw as Tyler's misuse of his power. For many, the scenario revived uncomfortable memories of Jackson's presidency. A major fight soon arose over the issue of tariffs.

Tariffs had been a hot topic in the country for more than twenty years. Supporters of these taxes, which are charged on goods that the Unites States imports from other countries, argued that tariffs were necessary for a number of reasons. By raising the price of imported products, U.S. goods became cheaper and therefore more appealing to consumers. As more and more factories sprang up in the North, their owners pushed for higher tariffs to help sell their goods. However, farmers in the South sold large amounts of cotton and other crops to foreign countries, including Great Britain. Southern farmers feared that high tariffs would lead those countries to set or raise tariffs of their own, damaging the South's international trade.

Southerners had so hated an 1828 bill that increased these controversial taxes that they called it the Tariff of Abominations. They felt strongly that the law favored northern factories while hurting southern farmers. In response to the outrage, some southern politicians began to argue for states' rights. The idea behind states' rights was that if the national government passed a law that an individual state considered unconstitutional, that state had the right to ignore the law. In 1832 South Carolina declared that it would refuse to obey the tariff laws. It even threatened to separate from the United States over the issues of tariffs and states' rights. Politicians fearful of a civil war rushed to repair the damage. They introduced a new, lower tariff. Government officials also supported U.S. businesses and farms by encouraging them to grow or produce as many goods as possible to avoid paying the tariffs. But the issue continued to trouble the nation and create tension between North and South.

Fillmore felt that tariffs were necessary to protect U.S. industry. During the ongoing depression, he also believed in using tariffs to raise money for the government treasury (a department in charge of public money). In 1841, with these ideas in mind, Fillmore began researching and writing a bill to raise national tariffs. He stressed that he saw the bill as a temporary measure to help the nation recover. He also argued that since other nations already taxed U.S. goods, the only way the country could stay competitive was by protecting its own industries with tariffs. It was a long fight. Facing repeated vetoes by President Tyler, Fillmore presented three separate bills on the subject. Finally, Fillmore's arguments—along with his positions as well-respected congressperson and head of the Ways and Means Committee—won the passage of the Whig Tariff Act of 1842.

President Tyler, who held the office from 1841 to 1845, used the presidential veto a lot. In this detail from a political cartoon of the 1840s, "Old Veto" Tyler holds up his veto sword.

———————————— ✧

Heading back to New York at the end of his term, Fillmore was ready to take a break from his congressional duties. He went home to pick up his law practice and other quieter pursuits. But he remained a local celebrity. A New York newspaper commented on the activities of the Buffalonian. The paper described him in glowing terms: "His features . . . are decidedly expressive and agreeable, and in or out of Congress there are few better looking men. . . . His talents are of a high grade. . . . His judgement is very clear, and . . . whatever he undertakes he will master. . . . He has many of the highest attributes of greatness, and is still a young man."

Fillmore's accomplishments impressed all who knew him. Many still encouraged Fillmore to run for offices such as New York governor or even vice president. While these possibilities sounded exciting, Fillmore wasn't sure that he was ready for them. The same modesty that he had felt as a young lawyer may have made him nervous about holding such high offices. Nevertheless, he started to warm up to the idea of the vice presidency in 1843. At the same time, however, Whigs began to disagree on who would be the best candidate. In the end, Fillmore failed to win the nomination.

Disappointed but not completely discouraged, Fillmore switched his focus. He began to concentrate on running for governor, as his supporters still wished him to do. But Senator Silas Wright defeated him in the October 1844 election. The loss—his first serious political setback—was an unexpected blow. Other Whigs did poorly that year too. Henry Clay lost the presidential race to Democrat James K. Polk—whom the elderly Andrew Jackson had supported. Under the circumstances, Fillmore resolved to take a real break from office and to enjoy family and professional life in Buffalo. Sticking to his plan, he refused a second run at governor in 1846.

BACK IN THE SPOTLIGHT

Despite Fillmore's intentions, politics soon called to him once again. In 1847 his supporters nominated him for New York State comptroller. The comptroller's job was to manage state finances. The office was an important one. The position's duties appealed to Fillmore, who still had fond memories of bookkeeping for Cheney. He entered the race and easily won the election. With Abigail at his side, he left Buffalo to take his seat in Albany.

Fillmore came up for the position of vice president again in 1848. The presidential nominee that year was Zachary Taylor. Taylor was a well-known war hero. Nicknamed Old Rough and Ready, he had never held any public office before. However, he was a strong-willed and charismatic man. Officially a Whig, he had relatively moderate views that the party hoped would appeal to both Whig and Democratic voters.

Fillmore won the vice-presidential nomination in June 1848. Eager to reclaim the presidency for the Whig Party, he immediately threw himself into campaigning against the Democratic candidate, Lewis Cass. His efforts, aided by the work of his fellow party members and by Taylor's popularity, paid off. Whigs across the country rejoiced when the Taylor-Fillmore team won in November. Fillmore was on his way to the nation's capital again—this time as its second-most-powerful leader.

This Whig campaign banner for the 1848 presidential election promotes Zachary Taylor for president and Millard Fillmore for vice president.

CHAPTER FIVE

"I DARE NOT SHRINK"

In the discharge of this duty, solemnly imposed upon me by the Constitution and by my oath of office, I shall shrink from no responsibility, and shall endeavor to meet events as they may arise with firmness, as well as with prudence and discretion.

—Millard Fillmore, 1850

Taylor and Fillmore took office in March 1849. Fillmore arrived in Washington alone that month. Abigail had been very ill and was not well enough to travel. As always, Fillmore missed his wife and kept in touch through letters. From his living quarters at the Willard Hotel, he wrote to her, "How lonesome this room is in your absence. . . . I can hardly bear to sit down." But he soon found plenty to occupy his time and his thoughts. First and foremost, he was finally able to meet the man with whom he had been elected. Until reaching Washington, Taylor and Fillmore had exchanged a few letters but had never met. About one week before the inauguration, they came face-to-face for the first time. Fillmore was probably unsure of whether this untested partnership would succeed. But he would soon learn as events of the time came into play and presented the president and vice president with their first big challenge.

SLAVERY

When Taylor and Fillmore took office, slavery was the most controversial topic in the country. Tensions surrounding the subject had been growing steadily since the early 1800s. Slavery itself was nothing new. Ever since the 1600s, residents of the American colonies—and later of the United States—had purchased African slaves to work the fields of plantations (large farms in the South). This enormous source of labor was very important to southern business.

PICKING COTTON ON A GEORGIA PLANTATION.

✧ ————
This print from the early 1800s shows slave children as well as adults picking cotton on a plantation in Georgia.

One of the biggest issues of the 1848 election had been slavery. Fillmore opposed slavery—a position that some Whigs had feared could ruin his and Taylor's chances in the South. But Taylor was from the South and owned more than one hundred slaves himself. This combination of an anti-slavery northerner and a slaveholding southerner had appealed to many voters.

However, more and more Americans—especially in the North—came to feel that slavery was cruel and inhuman. Some said that it violated the rights of "life, liberty, and the pursuit of happiness" promised in the Constitution. These people, called abolitionists, wanted to abolish, or end, slavery in the entire country. But southerners protested that their farms and businesses would collapse without slave labor. As the problem intensified, it threatened to divide the nation. States decided for themselves whether to allow slavery. If the fragile balance of anti-slaveholding and slaveholding states was upset, many people believed deep unrest—or even civil war—would be the result.

However, the issue raised its head again not long after the presidential inauguration. The United States had recently won the Mexican-American War (1846–1848). As a result, the United States had gained vast amounts of land in the Southwest, including California, Texas, and New Mexico. In June the question arose as to whether to add California to the country as a state or a territory. If it became a state, it would be either free or slaveholding. This would shatter the balance between the North and the South.

Taylor hoped to see California become a state. Despite his southern roots, he also supported its entry as a free state. As slaveholding states saw themselves about to sink into the minority, the uproar grew. Southerners argued strongly for their economic needs. Meanwhile, abolitionists—including free blacks in the North and former slaves who had escaped the South—continued to speak out with equal passion against slavery. By December, as California inched toward statehood and Congress fought over the issue, Taylor found himself in the midst of a political thunderstorm. Over the next six months, the commotion only grew as the same questions arose regarding other potential states, such as Oregon and Minnesota.

COMPROMISE AND CALAMITY

Throughout this unrest, Fillmore was hardly sitting idly by. In 1850 he began serving as president of the Senate. This was one of his duties as vice president. Overseeing the Senate aroused Fillmore's old modesty. He asked the senators for their help. He said that "you will not doubt my sincerity when I assure that I assume the responsible duties

SCENE IN UNCLE SAM'S SENATE.

This political cartoon makes fun of the Senate debate over admitting California as a free state. Vice President Fillmore, as the president of the Senate (top, center), waves his gavel at the unruly senators.

of this chair, with a conscious lack of experience, and a just appreciation that I shall often need your friendly suggestions."

As Senate president, Fillmore guided the heated debate on slavery and states' rights. Like many observers, he feared that if the issue could not be settled, southern states would secede, or separate themselves from the rest of the country. Faced with this possibility, he was determined to fight for the nation's unity. He was also convinced that the Senate could reach a solution that would please both the North and the South. Taylor, however, was less interested in compromise. He hoped to avoid as much of the conflict as possible.

Partly because of their differing political views, the relationship between president and vice president had grown strained since their election. Fillmore suspected that Taylor did not trust him enough to give him big responsibilities. He complained that the president ignored his advice. But, while the situation frustrated Fillmore, he was still fiercely loyal to the Whig Party. To avoid embarrassing or weakening the party, he took care not to criticize Taylor openly.

Meanwhile, Fillmore remained committed to his duties. He continued to oversee the Senate efforts to agree on the slavery issue. In January 1850, Senator Henry Clay presented a bill intended to settle the question. It called for antislavery measures, including allowing California to become a free state and ending the slave trade in Washington, D.C. Northern abolitionists welcomed these suggestions. However, Clay also put forth points meant to please the South. He proposed that new territories stay neutral on slavery until they became states. If and when they did, he said, they could decide the matter for themselves. More important to most southerners, he suggested the passage and strict enforcement of a Fugitive Slave Act. This law ensured that slaves who had escaped to the North would be arrested and returned to their owners.

Despite Clay's careful plan to please everyone, debate raged in Congress. Both North and South argued that the deal was too generous to the other side. Taylor also opposed the bill—called the Compromise of 1850 or the Omnibus Bill. Although Fillmore was careful to remain mostly neutral in his public statements, he privately favored the measure. He was prepared to throw his support—and his reputation—behind it if necessary.

But before the opposing sides in Congress could agree upon the compromise, events took a new and disastrous turn. On the Fourth of July in 1850, President Taylor suddenly came down with a high fever and took to his bed. Less than one week later, on July 9, he died. Fillmore decided not to offer a formal inauguration speech in view of the sad occasion. Instead, he said a few words, took the oath of office, and became the thirteenth president of the United States. Later in the day, members of Congress listened to a message sent by President Fillmore:

> *A great man has fallen among us and a whole country is called to an occasion of . . . deep, and general mourning. . . . I appeal to you to aid me . . . in the discharge of the duties from which . . . I dare not shrink.*

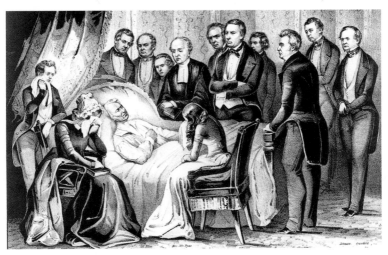

A dying Taylor was surrounded by mourners. His death in 1850 thrust Fillmore into the presidency.

AN UNWANTED PROMOTION

Taylor's sudden death had given Fillmore little time to prepare himself for the presidency. The burden of the office
weighed heavily on his shoulders. An uncle sympathized
with his concern, writing, "While I would feel to congratu-
late you . . . My Dear & Excellent Nephew my heart is [full
of] anxiety for you in view of the vast responsibility so
unexpectantly [fallen] upon you." With these thoughts
hanging over him, Fillmore moved into the White House
so recently lived in by Taylor. He eagerly looked forward to
Abigail joining him. Her health had improved at last. She
traveled to Washington as soon as possible.

Fillmore's first duty as president was to choose a cabinet
(the group of aides who would be his closest advisers).
Taylor's cabinet was not especially fond of Fillmore nor he
of them. They resigned and allowed him to start fresh with
people he chose. Fillmore asked his old friend Daniel
Webster to be secretary of state, one of the highest cabinet
positions. Webster was a skillful and intelligent politician.
He would be a valuable help to Fillmore. At fifty years old,
Fillmore was still a young man for the job of president. In
addition, Fillmore offered a post to his old law partner
Nathan K. Hall. Hall had gone on from the law firm in
Buffalo to pursue a political career of his own. Many of the
other members of the cabinet—who were from both the
North and the South—favored the compromise bill so dear
to Fillmore's own heart.

As the shock and uncertainty surrounding Taylor's death
began to lessen, the bill came back to the forefront.
Disagreement and bitter conflict still swirled around the
issue. However, Fillmore remained firmly convinced of its

This photograph of Nathan K. Hall (right) was probably taken while Hall served as postmaster general in President Fillmore's cabinet from 1850 to 1852. Fillmore had hired Hall as a law clerk in 1826.

———————— ✧

value. As president, he openly stated his position. He was prepared to fight for it. In September 1850, the measure finally passed. President Fillmore officially signed into law the bill that he had quietly supported as vice president.

Even after its passage, the law remained controversial. Many northerners—including Whigs—criticized Fillmore. They were especially angry that he had agreed to the

Fillmore signed the Fugitive Slave Act into law in September 1850. Copies of the controversial new law circulated all over the United States.

Fugitive Slave Act. Some historians believe that Abigail tried to convince her husband to change or veto that part of the bill. But Fillmore defended his actions. He claimed that the Fugitive Slave Act was in keeping with the Constitution's requirement that states respect one another's laws. In addition, he firmly believed that the act was necessary to satisfy southern states and that keeping the country together was the most important goal of all. He wrote to Secretary of State Webster, "God knows that I [hate] slavery, but it is an existing evil, for which we are not responsible, and we must endure it . . . till we can get rid of it without destroying the last hope of free government in the world."

STORMY SEAS

Only a few weeks passed before the first major protest against the compromise took place. In October 1850, a group of abolitionists in Pennsylvania attempted to free a fugitive slave. Police tried to form an armed group of local

In this print from 1850, white men hunt a group of African Americans. The Fugitive Slave Act allowed European Americans to treat all African Americans as fugitive slaves. Many free African Americans became slaves this way.

citizens to help hold the captive. But their efforts failed. When a mob stormed the jail and released the prisoner, Pennsylvania judges asked Fillmore to allow national troops to enforce the Fugitive Slave Act when necessary. Fillmore felt forced to uphold the law. He agreed to the judges' request, despite renewed outcry from abolitionists.

One month later, the issue nearly erupted into a crisis. A group of southern governors held a convention in Nashville, Tennessee. They were still angry over what they viewed as the compromise's insulting and unfair treatment of the South. The governors hoped to call for secession. Knowing that such an outcome was possible, Fillmore had already ordered that troops travel to the South in case of rebellion. When South Carolina's governor questioned Fillmore about this move, the president defended it. He declared that, as commander in chief of the armed forces, it was his constitutional right to use troops if he felt it was necessary. When the convention began, the combination of Fillmore's strong stance and the support of southern Whigs resulted in no vote to secede. The divided country narrowly avoided conflict yet again.

On December 2, President Fillmore gave his first address to Congress. He again tried to calm the uproar over the compromise. He urged his listeners to support the law and to put peace and stability above political disagreements. He said:

> I believe those measures [of the bill] to have been required by the circumstances. . . . They were adopted in the spirit of [agreement], and for the purpose of [agreement]. I believe that a great

majority of our fellow citizens sympathize in that spirit, and that purpose, and . . . that the American people, bound together by . . . common traditions, still cherish the Union of their fathers.

With this statement, the turbulent year of 1850 drew to a close. Fillmore remained certain that the compromise bill had helped to prevent war between the states. But political war still raged within the party and the Congress, and Fillmore still stood in the center of the conflict.

In 1851 the arrest, escape, and trial of fugitive slave Anthony Burns (above) caused riots in Boston, Massachusetts.

CHAPTER SIX

STRUGGLES AND CARES

Let us hope that . . .
this venerated constitution, and this glorious
Union, may endure forever.
—Millard Fillmore, 1849

Fillmore's first six months in office had been long and challenging. A break was not yet in sight. Discontent with and disobedience of the Fugitive Slave Act continued in the North. Some northern states passed laws meant to interfere with enforcement of the Fugitive Slave Act. But the U.S. Supreme Court ruled that these laws were unconstitutional.

In February 1851, a group of free blacks and abolitionists in Boston, Massachusetts, freed a fugitive slave who was imprisoned there. Fillmore lost hope that such violent confrontations were over. Meanwhile, an international dispute also arose. It gave President Fillmore his first contact with foreign policy issues.

INTERNATIONAL RELATIONS

After the Mexican-American War, further complications had arisen between the two nations. U.S. officials and businesspeople were pressing for permission to build a railroad across the Isthmus of Tehuantepec. The Isthmus is a narrow land bridge that lies in Mexican territory between the Gulf of Tehuantepec and the Bay of Campeche. Like the great Erie Canal, the railroad would be valuable to shipping and industry. President Fillmore strongly supported the ambitious project. Secretary of State Webster traveled to Mexico to propose possible deals. But Mexican officials were reluctant to agree. Meanwhile, Mexico demanded protection from raids into its territory by Native Americans from the north. This protection had been part of the treaty that had ended the war. But the treaty did not specify the exact terms. The Mexican government claimed that if such raids did take place, the United States should pay Mexico for any damages. When Mexico refused to agree to the railroad, the United States responded by threatening to withhold the requested payments.

Much of the Mexican population was firmly against an agreement with the United States. In fact, the opposition was so strong that if the two countries were to sign a treaty, war with or revolution against the Mexican government seemed dangerously possible. Making one last attempt to find a solution, Fillmore wrote a letter to the Mexican president in March 1851. In the letter, he urged the Mexican leader to reconsider. The letter hinted at a threat, suggesting that the United States might feel the need to use military force to settle the matter. The letter was unlike most of Fillmore's communication. It showed a harder, less compassionate side of the president. Fillmore may have wanted the glory of settling the dispute with Mexico. Or he may have felt that without such a strong statement, war truly might have resulted. But no treaty was reached during Fillmore's presidency.

Another tricky international issue involved Cuba. A small island that lies just ninety miles from the coast of Florida, Cuba was a Spanish colony. Some Cubans wished to win their freedom from Spain. And some Americans—with the United States' own fight for independence not long past—supported the freedom movement on the island. Many Americans saw the island as a tempting prize for the United States. President Polk had tried unsuccessfully to buy Cuba during his administration. Cuba would provide the United States with rich farmland and a valuable port on the Caribbean Sea. But it was still active in the slave trade. This appealed to southerners still wishing to buy more slaves.

In August 1851, Narciso López, a Venezuelan immigrant living in New York, recruited a group of men—many of them Americans—to sail to Cuba. The plan, once there, was to spur a revolution that would end in the island's independence. López had tried a similar feat twice before but had failed on both occasions. One attempt had fallen apart even before the force could sail from New York. Another had reached Cuba but met with a swift defeat. This time López and his band of more than four hundred men reached Cuba again. But Spanish troops promptly attacked the invaders. Many of López's men died in the battle that followed. The Spanish

This political cartoon accuses López of being more interested in stealing money from the Cuban towns he conquered than in leading a political revolution.

✧ ————————————

captured López and publicly executed him. They threw the rest of the force into jails in Cuba and in Spain.

The violent incident caused a massive outcry among Americans. Angry citizens demanded the release of the prisoners and renewed the call for Cuban independence. But Fillmore was torn. As had been the case during the *Caroline* affair, U.S. interference in Cuba violated neutrality agreements. Fillmore felt great sorrow for the fate of the American captives, but they had broken both national and international law. The president was well aware of how delicate the situation was. Not only did he have to smooth things over with Spain, but he needed to reassure Britain and France—both of which had colonies in the Caribbean—that the United States did not want to take over any of their land.

Fillmore agreed to negotiate with Spain for the release of the prisoners. In time they were freed. But, in his next speech to Congress in December 1851, the president expressed his own strong disapproval of the expedition itself. He said that Americans who broke "the law of nations and the laws of the United States" should not expect their government to defend them. He went on to say that "[i]f we desire to maintain our respectability among the nations of the earth, it behooves us to enforce steadily and sternly the neutrality acts passed by Congress." Nevertheless, Fillmore could be proud that he had successfully guided a very delicate situation to a peaceful conclusion.

THE NATIONAL SCENE

Although his experience with foreign policy was often frustrating, Fillmore made progress within the United States. Most of his efforts focused on developing U.S. business and industry. These projects included building harbors and lighthouses for coastal, riverfront, or Great Lakes cities. In addition, he supported national funding to build railroads. Workers laid many miles of track during his term. Fillmore also wanted to expand and update the military, returning to an interest in defense that he had voiced during the *Caroline* controversy in 1837.

A smaller change that had far-reaching effects was the lowering of postal rates. The cost of mailing a letter within the country fell several cents. The use of the mail by both businesses and individuals expanded significantly as a result. The government would not raise the rate again for decades.

First Family

For Fillmore, one of the greatest highlights of the presidency was being with his family. After Abigail had come to the capital, Powers and Abby had joined their parents there. The family lived together for the first time in many years.

For a couple that had lived comfortably but not lavishly, the elegant presidential mansion was quite a change. But as the Fillmores grew accustomed to living there, they soon began adding personal touches to their new home. One of the most lasting changes was in perfect keeping with Fillmore and Abigail's common love of reading. Both were amazed to find that the residence lacked books. The couple worked together to request and receive funds from Congress to establish a permanent White House library. Abigail had a room on the second floor of the house carefully redecorated and filled with close to one thousand books. The works included books by authors ranging from William Shakespeare to Daniel Webster. From then on, the library was one of the family's favorite spots. They enjoyed chatting or playing the game backgammon there in the evenings. Abigail especially loved the room.

As before, the capital's hectic social scene intimidated Abigail. Her health—while improved—was still fragile. As a result, it was her daughter who hosted the many receptions, dinners, and other events that drew visitors to the president's home every week. Abby was by then eighteen years old. She was a charming, popular young woman who loved parties and fine clothes. She also provided pleasant company for her parents. Having had a good education, she was well-read, fluent in French and Spanish, and a skilled musician. At the end of her father's workday, she often soothed his nerves by playing piano or harp for him in the library.

At the White House, Abby (left) enjoyed serving as the hostess in place of her sickly mother. Powers (right) continued to work for his father as he had in Buffalo.

Powers was a great help to his father as well. He had been working in the Buffalo law office. But after Fillmore became president, Powers served as his father's personal assistant, handling letters and other daily business.

The Fillmores recorded a quiet but historic first in 1850. That year Fillmore's father—who was by then more than eighty years old—joined them for a short stay. Nathaniel's visit marked the first time that a president had received his father as a White House guest. It was a happy occasion for the entire First Family.

*By the end of 1851,
President Fillmore had
decided not to run
for reelection.*

FADING HOPES

During Fillmore's presidency, Whigs had suffered defeats in elections around the country. Fillmore feared that his party was losing strength. In December 1851, he privately decided not to run for reelection. While he was proud of the Compromise of 1850, he knew that it had made him widely unpopular, greatly damaging his chances at a second term. In addition, he found the idea of returning to Buffalo and leading a quiet life quite appealing.

Another factor in Fillmore's decision was Webster's status as a likely Whig candidate for president. Fillmore had full faith in his secretary of state's abilities and would have been comfortable leaving the office in his hands. But as the nominating convention neared, support for

Webster—who had never been popular in the South—
began to weaken. Party members feared that Webster's
nomination would cost them the White House. They
began urging Fillmore to run. He finally agreed.

But doubts about Fillmore's chances for victory also
arose—due in part, as Fillmore had expected, to the controversial compromise. Fillmore's disadvantage also
stemmed from his unwillingness to launch a major reelection campaign. Influential Whigs turned to General
Winfield Scott as the party's last hope. He had the dou-
ble advantage of being a southerner and being yet another popular war hero. With three potential nominees, the
Whigs were deeply divided. At the nominating convention in June 1852, after lengthy debate, Scott won the
party's presidential nomination.

The Whigs nominated
General Winfield Scott to
run for president in 1852.

Fillmore suddenly became a lame duck. This is the unflattering nickname for a president who, after winning neither renomination nor reelection, is just waiting for his time in office to end. During this period, one of Fillmore's final acts as president brought him back into international affairs. In November 1852, he approved the first U.S. trade mission to Japan. At the time, Japan did not allow foreigners into its ports. However, European nations and the United States saw Japan as an important potential trading partner as well as a valuable gateway to Asia. Led by Matthew C. Perry, the U.S. expedition would eventually lead to the opening of Japan to foreign trade.

———————————— ◇ ————————————

Matthew C. Perry meets with Japanese leaders in 1853.

PARTING

Scott was up against Democrat Franklin Pierce in the 1852 election. Like Scott, Pierce had been an officer in the Mexican-American War. He had served as a congressman for several years. The public generally saw him as a moderate politician. As a presidential candidate, he had the complete support of his party. The Democrats were eager to reclaim the presidency after an absence of twelve years. Nevertheless, Whigs held tight to their own hopes.

But in the end, the growing divide between northern and southern Whigs was too great to overcome. On November 2, Pierce won the presidential election in a landslide. Yet Fillmore expressed no regret. He even sounded rather grateful to be leaving. He said that "I should be no more harassed with the cares of state, or worn down with professional labors." While this comment may well have hidden some disappointment, it was probably largely true. Fillmore could look forward to a peaceful retirement in the familiar surroundings of Buffalo, with his beloved Abigail at his side.

Fillmore remained an influential man after his presidency.

CHAPTER SEVEN

THE ELDER STATESMAN

I aspire to nothing more, and shall retire
from the exciting scenes of political strife
to the quiet enjoyments of my own
family and fireside.
—Millard Fillmore, 1842

On March 4, 1853, Fillmore and Abigail attended Franklin Pierce's inauguration ceremony. The day was cold. Rain and snow filled the gray skies. But even as the gathered crowd shivered in the wind, it warmed Fillmore's heart to hear Pierce declare his intention to uphold the Compromise of 1850. Fillmore regarded Pierce as a good and capable man and believed that he would keep his promises.

Fillmore and Abigail planned to leave Washington within the week to begin a trip through the southern United States. But then Abigail's health declined further, perhaps made worse by the bad weather at Pierce's inauguration. Running a fever and finding it hard to breathe, she took to her bed. Fillmore delayed the couple's travel plans. He stayed by his wife's side, reading to her and trying to make her as comfortable as possible. Fillmore called doctors and nurses to care for the patient. But her condition still worsened. After three agonizing weeks, Abigail died on the morning of March 30, 1853.

Fillmore was utterly shattered by the loss of his beloved wife. He described the loss in letters to friends and family. He recalled that "for twenty-seven years, my entire married life, I was always greeted with a happy smile." As the sad news spread, messages of sympathy poured in from around the country. Out of respect for the ex-president, the Senate canceled its session for the day. Many members of the government visited Fillmore to offer their condolences.

On March 31, Fillmore, Abby, and Powers left Washington for Buffalo. Abigail was buried there on the first of April. Home at last, Fillmore could hardly summon the will to go on. "I have felt no desire to do anything," he wrote to Dorothea Dix, a family friend. "The light of the house is gone; and I can never hope to enjoy life again."

TRIALS AND TRAVELS

As Fillmore slowly struggled to recover from Abigail's death, he also witnessed upheavals in other areas of his life. Defeats in the 1852 elections had been the final blow to the already weakened Whig Party. It dissolved not long afterward.

A further threat to the political ideals dear to Fillmore arose in January 1854. Senator Stephen A. Douglas of Illinois proposed the Nebraska Bill. The measure called for giving the new territories of Nebraska and Kansas the

Illinois senator Stephen A. Douglas defended his Nebraska Bill in many public debates. They included a series of debates in 1858 with future U.S. president Abraham Lincoln. These famous debates are known as the Lincoln-Douglas Debates.

power to choose whether to allow slavery. This proposal threatened to undo the careful work of the Compromise of 1850. It also went against the Missouri Compromise, which stated that no region north of an agreed-upon line would permit slavery. The bill passed in March, much to the dismay of abolitionists. Fillmore worried over the dangers of the bill and of threatening the delicate truce that still held between North and South.

Oregon Territory

Minnesota Territory

Nebraska Territory

Utah Territory

California

Kansas Territory

public land

New Mexico Territory

Oklahoma

Texas

PACIFIC OCEAN

Millard Fillmore's United States, 1854

Slavery permitted

Slavery prohibited

Decision left to territories

MEXICO

That same month, Fillmore decided to take the trip southward that he and Abigail had not been able to take. Given the timing, some observers believed that Fillmore had a political motive in making the journey. They suspected that he might be planning to speak out against the Nebraska Bill. Others were convinced that it was a leisure tour. But whatever Fillmore's intentions may have been, his speeches to southern audiences were relatively neutral. He restated his faith in the compromise, but he spent most of his time enjoying a series of receptions, dinners, and parades in his honor throughout the region. A marching band escorted him through the streets of Louisville, Kentucky. Girls scattered his path with flowers in Montgomery, Alabama. A row of trains blew their whistles in greeting in Atlanta, Georgia. Fillmore returned home refreshed and with renewed faith in his fellow Americans.

Meanwhile, in the wake of the Whig collapse, two new parties formed to take its place. They were the Republican and the American parties. Choosing between the two groups, which both tried to sweep up the remnants of the Whigs, Fillmore chose to support the American Party. This party was nicknamed the Know-Nothings because its members met in secret and claimed to "know nothing" about the meetings. The party was strongly anti-Catholic and anti-immigrant. Fillmore did not like either of these views. However, he based his choice on practicality. He believed that only the Know-Nothings had any real chance of repairing the divide between the North and the South.

Fillmore followed current events eagerly. He had retired from law as well as politics. Yet he had discovered that he found all the rest and relaxation a little boring after a life-

*To appeal to young voters, the Know-Nothing Party used
this image of a fashionably dressed youth.*

———————————— ✧ ————————————

time of work. His attention was pulled away from politics
in July 1854 when twenty-two-year-old Abby suddenly died
of the disease cholera. Coming only a year after Abigail's
death, this second loss was devastating to Fillmore as well
as to Powers. In addition, father and daughter had been
planning a long trip to Europe together. Friends urged
Fillmore to make the journey alone, hoping that it might

lift his spirits. But he could not bring himself to go. He explained that "the more agreeable the journey, the deeper would be my regret that she could not share it with me. Every pleasure would be tinged with melancholy and every joy with a secret sorrow. I could not endure it. I must wait."

In January 1855, Fillmore was still reeling from the shock of Abby's death six months earlier. He nevertheless announced that he would seek the Know-Nothings' presidential nomination. The party had won elections in several states. It seemed to be a growing force. In addition, many people had urged Fillmore to run. They felt that his moderation and experience would make him a strong candidate. He rather reluctantly agreed to run.

Shortly thereafter, in March 1855, Fillmore finally gathered the energy to take his European tour. Boarding a steamship, he traveled to Great Britain, Ireland, France, and Italy. He also traveled beyond Europe to Egypt and Turkey. Along the way, he visited with world leaders such as the United Kingdom's Queen Victoria and with the pope.

During Fillmore's absence, the Know-Nothings nominated him for president. Fillmore's return ship docked in New York City in June 1856. On his way home to Buffalo, he did some unofficial campaigning. He delivered twenty-seven speeches, sharing his views on slavery, secession, the Nebraska Bill, and the duties of the president. He once again expressed his belief in preserving the nation's unity. He told crowds that he feared a Republican victory in the presidential election would lead to civil war. When he arrived in Buffalo near the end of July, his fellow Buffalonians greeted him with a warm outpouring of affection and respect.

But with this homecoming, Fillmore ended his cam-

This political cartoon supports Fillmore in the 1856 presidential campaign. Fillmore stands between feuding Republican candidate John C. Frémont (left) and Democratic candidate James Buchanan (right). Frémont opposes slavery, and Buchanan represents slaveholders.

✧

paigning. Between July and the election in November, the Republicans had time to gain strength. In addition, as Fillmore's speeches faded into memory, it became easier and easier for his opponents to interpret them unflatteringly. Fillmore's rivals accused him of supporting secession, being anti-Catholic, and reversing his opinion on various issues. Know-Nothing chances looked slim. When the elections rolled around, Democratic candidate James Buchanan easily beat Fillmore. The loss deeply disappointed Fillmore's supporters. Fillmore, however, accepted his defeat graciously. He planned to retreat from the political scene once and for all.

Even in retirement, Fillmore remained an active and popular member of the local social scene. In 1857 he went to a gathering at the home of a friend in Albany. The event's hostess was eager to introduce the ex-president to Caroline C. McIntosh. McIntosh was a wealthy widow also living in Albany. Fillmore and Caroline liked each other and soon became friends. On February 10, 1858, they married.

✧ ————————————
Fillmore's second wife, Caroline C. McIntosh, was a friendly companion in the final years of his life.

The newlyweds lived in this mansion on Niagara Square in Buffalo, New York.

——————————— ✧ ———————————

The love of Fillmore's life, nearly everyone agreed, had been Abigail. While he and Caroline were no doubt fond of each other, many observers suspected that their marriage was a friendly and convenient solution to problems that each of them had. Caroline was lonely but had a good deal of money. Fillmore had little income but was a charming companion. In any case, the Fillmores made contented partners. They lived in a large home in Buffalo, where they welcomed many guests to receptions and other social events.

"THE GATHERING STORM"

After Fillmore's presidential loss in 1856, he had spoken again of his belief that the turmoil between North and South was an omen of worse trouble to come. "I feel no regret," he said, "that I am relieved from . . . the laborious and thankless task of administering this government." He warned that "the [struggle] which disturbed the peace of the country in 1850 was . . . the muttering thunder and . . . the gathering storm [of an] . . . unholy rebellion."

The "gathering storm" that Fillmore predicted finally broke when the U.S. Civil War (1861–1865) erupted between the states of the North and the South. Fillmore watched with great sadness as the war tore the country apart.

———————————— ✧ ————————————

The Civil War started when Confederate (Southern) troops fired on Fort Sumter, South Carolina, in April 1861.

He watched with still greater sorrow as the bloody conflict left thousands of Americans dead and deprived many more of family and friends, as well as of property and possessions.

Before the war had begun, Fillmore and Caroline had entertained President Abraham Lincoln as a guest in Buffalo. Fillmore felt sympathy for Lincoln and the trials he faced

In this letter to Abraham Lincoln, dated December 16, 1861, Fillmore refers to the Civil War as "this unholy rebellion."

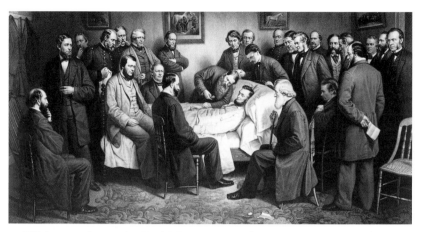

While at a play at the Ford Theatre in Washington, D.C., on April 14, 1865, Lincoln was shot in the back of his head. He died the next morning.

during the war. And he regretted his nation's loss when Lincoln was assassinated in 1865 as the war drew to a close.

Lincoln was far from the first—or last—famous guest of the Fillmores. For more than a decade longer, they opened their home to visitors of all kinds, including President Andrew Johnson in 1866. In the quiet retirement days that he had finally reached, Fillmore loved talking about politics, literature, and other topics in the comfort of his and Caroline's luxurious home.

A LIFE TO BE PROUD OF

In mid-February 1874, Fillmore suffered a sudden attack. It was probably a stroke. Whatever the cause, the episode left him partially paralyzed. Two weeks later, he had a second attack. He took to his bed. On March 8, 1874, Millard Fillmore died. The former president was laid to rest on March 12 at Buffalo's Forest Lawn Cemetery. He was buried

Millard and Abigail Fillmore are buried near their monument in Forest Lawn Cemetery in Buffalo, New York.

in a plot with Abigail and Abby, not far from his old friend Nathan K. Hall. Hall had died just six days earlier.

Fillmore's life and presidency were not the most dramatic in the nation's history. But they faithfully followed the principles that he always held dear. Hard work, education, and a deep patriotism brought Fillmore greater fame, admiration, and satisfaction than he could ever have dreamed of during his childhood in poverty. From his law practice to the many offices that he held in the public's service, he inspired respect and affection. He was a doting husband, a loving father, and a loyal friend. And his careful and practical acts as president helped stabilize the nation in a time of great turmoil. As one newspaper mourned after his death, "He leaves behind, alas! too few of his style of man."

AN UNCOMMON LEGACY

Although Fillmore is one of the least remembered U.S. presidents, his legacy lives on in a variety of ways. The earliest tributes showed up in the years during and following his presidency, when dozens of American parents named their children Millard Fillmore. Later, people remembered Fillmore for a few things that were not even true, such as the myth

✧ ────────────

This statue of Millard Fillmore by world-famous American sculptor Bryant Baker (1881–1970) stands outside City Hall in Buffalo, New York. The statue was part of the original design for City Hall, completed in 1932.

For the 205th anniversary of Fillmore's birthday, January 7, 2005, citizens of Buffalo, New York, including representatives of the Millard Fillmore College, decorated the Fillmore stone at Forest Lawn Cemetery.

─────── ✧

that the Fillmores installed the White House's first bathtub. A more genuine—but still rather unusual—honor is the Friends of Millard Fillmore Trivia Hunt, an annual research competition for students in the San Francisco, California, area.

But Fillmore's most lasting contributions and memorials speak of his lifetime of commitment to learning and reading. He and Abigail showed this commitment throughout their lives by founding libraries and by teaching others. In 1846 Fillmore became an honorary official at the University at Buffalo. And during his presidency, an unusual incident highlighted his respect for books. When a fire broke out at the Library of Congress, President Fillmore rushed to the scene and helped fight the blaze himself.

Almost one-half century after Fillmore's death, the night school of the University at Buffalo was founded and named Millard Fillmore College. The school's mission is to provide learning opportunities to nontraditional students who might not otherwise be able to go to college. This fitting honor commemorated Fillmore's belief in education's power to elevate anyone from struggle to success.

TIMELINE

1800   Millard Fillmore is born in Cayuga County, New York, on January 7.

1814   Fillmore becomes an apprentice to Benjamin Hungerford, a cloth maker in Sparta, New York.

1818   Fillmore works as a teacher.

1819   Fillmore enters New Hope Academy as a student and meets Abigail Powers. Fillmore works in the law offices of Judge Wood as a clerk.

1822   Fillmore moves to Buffalo and works as a law clerk for Asa Rice and Joseph Clary.

1823   Fillmore is admitted to the New York State Bar. He returns to East Aurora and opens a law firm.

1825   The Erie Canal is completed.

1826   Fillmore and Abigail Powers are married on February 5.

1828   Millard Powers Fillmore is born on April 25. In November Fillmore is elected to his first term in the New York State Assembly.

1829   Fillmore is reelected as assemblyman.

1830   The Fillmores move to Buffalo. Fillmore is elected to the assembly for a third time.

1831   Fillmore argues for a bill abolishing imprisonment for debt.

1832   Mary Abigail Fillmore is born on March 27. Fillmore is elected to the U.S. House of Representatives. Nathan K. Hall becomes a partner in Fillmore's law firm.

1834   The Anti-Masonic Party collapses and is replaced by the Whigs.

1836 Solomon G. Haven becomes the third partner in Fillmore's law firm, creating Fillmore, Hall, and Haven. Fillmore is reelected to Congress.

1837 Abigail joins Fillmore in the capital. An economic depression strikes the country. The *Caroline* affair takes place in December.

1840 William Henry Harrison is elected the first Whig president.

1841 Harrison dies in office, and Vice President John Tyler becomes president. Tyler quickly goes against Whig plans.

1842 With Fillmore's support, the Whig Tariff Act is passed.

1844 Fillmore runs for New York governor and loses.

1847 Fillmore is elected as New York comptroller.

1848 Fillmore is nominated for vice president. In November he and Zachary Taylor win the election. The United States wins the Mexican-American War and acquires the present-day states of New Mexico, Nevada, Utah, Arizona, and California.

1850 Fillmore serves as Senate president and supports the Omnibus Bill, including the controversial Fugitive Slave Act. On July 9, President Taylor dies. Fillmore becomes the thirteenth president of the United States. Fillmore sends troops to the South to prevent secession.

1851 Abolitionists in the North protest the Fugitive Slave Act. Fillmore tries to gain Mexican approval for the Tehuantepec railroad. After Narciso López's Cuban expedition ends in disaster in August, Fillmore agrees to negotiate with Spain.

1852 Fillmore agrees to run for reelection but loses the Whig nomination to Winfield Scott. Scott loses the election to Franklin Pierce.

1853 Pierce is inaugurated. Abigail Powers Fillmore dies on March 30.

1854 Senator Stephen A. Douglas introduces the Nebraska Bill. Fillmore tours the South. Abby dies of cholera in July.

1855 Fillmore takes a European tour. In his absence, the Know-Nothing Party nominates him for president. Fillmore helps to fund and create the Buffalo General Hospital.

1856 Fillmore loses the presidential election to James Buchanan.

1858 Fillmore marries Caroline C. McIntosh.

1861 The Civil War begins.

1865 The Civil War ends.

1867 Fillmore founds the Buffalo, New York, Society for the Prevention of Cruelty to Animals.

1874 Millard Fillmore dies on March 8.

SOURCE NOTES

7 W. L. Barre, *The Life and Public Services of Millard Fillmore* (1856, repr., New York: B. Franklin, 1971), 292.

9 Robert J. Scarry, *Millard Fillmore* (Jefferson, NC: McFarland & Company, 2001), 19.

11 Philip Kunhardt Jr., Philip Kunhardt III, and Peter W. Kunhardt, *The American President* (New York: Riverhead Books, 1999), 218.

12 Ibid., 220.

16 Scarry, 19.

19 Barre, 284.

23 Robert J. Rayback, *Millard Fillmore: Biography of a President* (Newtown, CT: American Political Biography Press, 1992), 10.

23 Scarry, 25.

25 Barre, 75.

25 Rayback, 13.

26 Scarry, 27.

31 Barre, 341.

35 Scarry, 37–38.

36 Barre, 124–125.

39 John J. Farrell, ed., *Zachary Taylor 1784–1850 [and] Millard Fillmore, 1800–1874; Chronology, Documents, Bibliographical Aids* (Dobbs Ferry, NY: Oceana Publications, 1971), 51.

43 Barre, 291.

48 Scarry, 98.

48 Ibid., 99.

48 Ibid., 106.

48 Ibid., 105.

49 Ibid., 108.

51 Ibid., 52.

53 Ibid., 65.

57 Ibid., 77.

61 Farrell, 78–79.

61 Elbert B. Smith, *The Presidencies of Zachary Taylor and Millard Fillmore* (Lawrence: University Press of Kansas, 1988), 160.

64–65 Barre, 312.

67 Scarry, 155.

68 Ibid., 169.

71 Ibid., 181.

72–73 Barre, 348–349.

75 Ibid., 314.

79 Farrell, 89.

85 Scarry, 237.

87 Barre, 285.

88 Scarry, 245.

88 Kunhardt, Kunhardt, and Kunhardt, 222.

94 Scarry, 267.

98 Ibid., 286.

98 Kunhardt, Kunhardt, and Kunhardt, 221.

101 Scarry, 338.

SELECTED BIBLIOGRAPHY

Barre, W. L. *The Life and Public Services of Millard Fillmore.* 1856. Reprint, New York: B. Franklin, 1971.

Farrell, John J., ed. *Zachary Taylor 1784–1850 [and] Millard Fillmore, 1800–1874; Chronology, Documents, Bibliographical Aids.* Dobbs Ferry, NY: Oceana Publications, 1971.

Gould, Lewis L., ed. *American First Ladies: Their Lives and Their Legacy.* New York: Routledge, 2001.

Grayson, Benson Lee. *The Unknown President: The Administration of President Millard Fillmore.* Washington, DC: University Press of America, 1981.

Kunhardt, Philip, Jr., Philip Kunhardt III, and Peter W. Kunhardt. *The American President.* New York: Riverhead Books, 1999.

Miller Center of Public Affairs. "Millard Fillmore." *American President.* 2003. http://www.americanpresident.org/history/ millardfillmore (February 6, 2004).

Rayback, Robert J. *Millard Fillmore: Biography of a President.* Newtown, CT: American Political Biography Press, 1992.

Scarry, Robert J. *Millard Fillmore.* Jefferson, NC: McFarland & Company, 2001.

Smith, Elbert B. *The Presidencies of Zachary Taylor and Millard Fillmore.* Lawrence: University Press of Kansas, 1988.

Snyder, Charles M. *The Lady and the President: The Letters of Dorothea Dix and Millard Fillmore.* Lexington: University Press of Kentucky, 1975.

White House. *Biography of Abigail Fillmore.* N.d. http://www .whitehouse.gov/history/firstladies/af13.html (February 6, 2004).

FURTHER READING AND WEBSITES

The American Presidency Project: 1st Annual Message, Millard Fillmore.
   http://www.presidency.ucsb.edu/ws/index.php?pid=29491
   Read the first State of the Union address that President Fillmore delivered to his country.

American President: Millard Fillmore
   http://www.americanpresident.org/history/millardfillmore/
   This site provides a biography of Millard Fillmore, vital statistics of the former president, and resources for more information.

Arnold, James R. *The Civil War*. Minneapolis: Lerner Publications Company, 2005.

Arnold, James R., and Roberta Wiener. *Divided in Two: The Road to Civil War, 1861*. Minneapolis: Lerner Publications Company, 2002.

Campbell, Kumari. *Cuba in Pictures*. Minneapolis: Lerner Publications Company, 2005.

Childress, Diana. *The War of 1812*. Minneapolis: Lerner Publications Company, 2004.

Cleveland, Will, and Mark Alvarez. *Yo, Millard Fillmore!* Brookfield, CT: Millbrook Press, 1997.

Feldman, Ruth Tenzer. *The Mexican-American War*. Minneapolis: Lerner Publications Company, 2004.

Gelman, Amy. *New York*. Minneapolis: Lerner Publications Company, 2002.

Harvey, Bonnie Carman. *Daniel Webster: Liberty and Union, Now and Forever*. Berkeley Heights, NJ: Enslow Publishers, 2001.

Landau, Elaine. *The President's Work: A Look at the Executive Branch*. Minneapolis: Lerner Publications Company, 2004.

Lindop, Edmund. *Presidents by Accident*. New York: Franklin Watts, 1991.

Roberts, Jeremy. *Zachary Taylor*. Minneapolis: Lerner Publications Company, 2005.

INDEX

African Americans (blacks), 64, 71. *See also* Africans; slavery
Africans, 62
Anti-Masonic Party, 32–33, 34, 35, 44, 45, 46

Bank of the United States, 45. *See also* Jackson, Andrew
Buchanan, James, 42; and 1856 presidential election, 95, 106

Caroline affair, 52, 78, 79
Cass, Lewis, 59
Cheney, Zaccheus, 16, 20–21, 58
Civil War, 98–100
civil war (threat of), 56, 63, 94
Clary, Joseph, 25, 105
Clay, Henry, 44, 58, 66
Cuba, 77–78. *See also* Fillmore, Millard: foreign policy of

Democratic Party, 44, 59, 95
Douglas, Stephen A., 88–89

Erie Canal, 40, 76
Europe: France, 78, 94; Great Britain (United Kingdom), 9–10, 52, 55, 78, 94; Ireland, 94; and Revolutionary War, 9–10; Spain, 77–79; and U.S. tariffs and trade, 55–56; and War of 1812, 38, 52

Fillmore, Abigail Powers (first wife), 17–18, 24, 27–28, 29, 33–36, 37, 46–47, 48, 58, 61; death of, 88, 92; as First Lady, 68, 70, 84, 87–88, 92, 97, 100, 103
Fillmore, Caroline C. McIntosh (second wife), 96–97, 99, 100
Fillmore, Mary Abigail (Abby) (daughter), 41, 47, 48–49, 81, 88, 101; death of, 92, 94

Fillmore, Millard: accomplishments and legacy of, 100–101, 102–103; and Anti-Masonic Party, 33, 35, 44, 45, 46; and bankruptcy legislation, 37–38; birth and childhood, 10–12, 13–15, 16–17, 18; and cabinet, 68–69; and *Caroline* affair, 52, 78, 79; and Compromise of 1850, 68–69, 70–73, 88; death of, 100–101; domestic policy of, 68–73, 79; early apprenticeships of, 7–8, 13–15, 16–17, 18, 19–20; education of, 10, 11, 17; and 1856 presidential election, 94–95; as elder statesman, 87–88, 92; and family, 28–29; finances of, 13–16, 18, 20–21, 23–26, 27; foreign policy of, 5, 75–79, 84; and Fugitive Slave Act, , 69–71, 75; as lame duck president, 84–85; as law clerk, 20, 23, 25; as lawyer, 26–28, 46, 50–51; loss and grief, 88, 93–94; love and marriages of, 17–18, 24, 27–28, 96–97; as New York State assemblyman, 33, 34–36, 37–39, 43, 45; as New York State comptroller, 58; presidency of, 67–73, 75–84; as president of the Senate, 64–66; as Representative, 41, 46–47, 50–57, 78, 79; and slavery, 62, 63–64, 65–66, 71, 89, 94, 95; and tariffs and trade, 56; as teacher, 22–23, 24, 25, 103; and U.S. Civil War, 98–100; vice presidency, 61–66; and vice presidential nomination, 57–59; and Ways and Means Committee, 54, 56; and Whig Party, 46–47, 50, 54–55, 56–57, 58, 59, 60, 63, 66, 69–70, 71, 72, 82–83, 105, 106
Fillmore, Millard Powers (son), 29, 34, 35, 46, 47, 80, 81, 88
Fillmore, Nathaniel (father), 9, 10, 12–13, 16, 20, 29, 81
Fillmore, Phoebe (mother), 9, 10, 11, 29; death of 39

❖ 110 ❖

ABOUT THE AUTHOR

Alison Behnke is an author and editor of children's books. She also enjoys traveling and learning about U.S. and world history. Her other books include *Pope John Paul II, Italians in America,* and *North Korea in Pictures.*